The Lazy Person's Common Sense Guide to the Business of Lawn Care

How to Become a More Laid-back Lawn Expert and Enjoy the Grass!

By Jamie Raines

Table of Contents

Introduction 4

Chapter 1 – Creating a Lawn 8

    A Lawn from Seed 9

    Turfing a Lawn 12

    Renovating an Old Lawn 16

Chapter 2 – Feeding a Lawn and Keeping It Healthy 20

Chapter 3 – Lawn Pests and How to Deal with Them 26

Chapter 4 – The Four Seasons 33

    Spring 33

    Summer 38

    Autumn 41

    Winter 43

Chapter 5 – Cutting the Lawn 45

Chapter 6 – Non-grass Lawns 53

Conclusion 56

Introduction

There are any number of books and guides on the subject of Lawn Maintenance and Lawn Care. Think of this book as a series of notes to help you to both understand and look after your lawn as well as telling you WHY you are doing it... and it is not just about grass.

Camomile lawns, mossy lawns, flower lawns, clover lawns, wildflower lawns and even Astroturf lawns. They all require different specialist knowledge and we shall briefly discuss them in a later chapter but the main 'thrust' of this book is the good old-fashioned grass lawn in its various forms and sizes.

The traditional grass lawn has been around for many years. In fact, it has been a feature of most gardens since the invention of the lawnmower because without some sort of mechanical cutter, it would be impossible to even contemplate a sort of carpet-like, close-cropped patch of grass which seems to be the feature of over 90% of all domestic gardens.

It is one of those aspects of the garden which, in spite of changes in taste and fashion, has managed to hold on against the onslaught of everything from decking to coloured paving, ponds, water features and for the other transient crazes which gardening has become prone to in the last hundred years.

Nowadays we have lawn experts who will tell you the correct mixture of grasses, how many times a lawn should be cut, and even how to feed it. Yes, to many obsessive lawn fanatics it seems that a lawn can be treated with the same amount of care and love that one would normally reserve for a pet dog or cat.

A well maintained grass lawn can not only be a great addition to a family's leisure time, especially if there are children who need space to run around and play, but it is also very attractive and certainly the cheapest form of ground covering.

You may assume that it is maintenance free – after all, it is *only* grass – but if you're looking for something natural that will not only enhance your garden but also your property, then there is nothing like a beautifully cut and striped deep and soft green lawn to do the job! That inevitably means maintenance and work.

Speaking of changing fashions, there was a time when a family's lawn was indeed cut to be immaculate and mostly decorative, which meant that it wasn't fulfilling any practical function and for all intents and purposes was no more than a showpiece.

Today, a proper lawn looks slightly less formal than its cousin from the previous generation. Those lawn stripes which were such an essential feature of the old school lawn are no more than a distant memory because instead of the old cylinder mowers we now tend to use those rotary mowers which are designed just to cut the grass rather than create a work of art.

The only stripes you tend to see nowadays are on cricket and football pitches, but no doubt there will come a time when fashions change yet again and we'll be back to striped or chequerboard grass.

Fifty years ago there was grass – just grass. Which meant that if the lawn grass was cut to a height of say 10mm, it could be prickly and hard to sit on. These days there are many strains of ornamental hybrid grasses which are bred for all sorts of qualities, ranging from looks to being hard wearing. The various new blends of grasses are suitable for sunny lawns, shady lawns and even damp lawns. In short, what used to be a small square of grass can be a bit of gardener's specialist 'minefield'.

Apart from the recreational aspect of the lawn and the undoubted artistic merit of some of the most extreme manicured and cosseted lawns, they are not only an integral part of a garden's overall canvas by setting off and providing a contrast to all the colour in a garden *but* they also attract wildlife... especially birds.

It is for these reasons that a properly maintained lawn can be a great asset which deserves our attention.

This book is going to cover all aspects of lawn maintenance, including actually laying down the lawn using turf or seed, caring for it and mowing it, together with a chapter on how to treat it with the changing seasons. There will even be a chapter on how to deal with lawn pests, ranging from weeds to ants and moles!

We shall also be learning about those 'non-grass' lawns mentioned above... so whether you are an amateur of whether gardening is your business, all the knowledge you need is in the next few pages.

This is no "Lawn Care for Dummies" but it is here to help you to understand and enjoy your lawn – without the worry and stress.

Chapter 1 – Creating a Lawn

The foundation of any traditional garden, and therefore the most important element, is a grass lawn. With a little basic knowledge a lawn is very easy to establish and maintain, although climate variations will decide on the ongoing upkeep and maintenance.

As with most things, when establishing a lawn it is the preparation which is both the most important and which takes the most time.

When the new site for a lawn is being prepared there are several basic issues which need to be addressed and which will ensure the longevity and appearance of the lawn. Unwanted roots and weeds should be removed, and in order to make doubly sure that there will not be resurgence of weeds, it is best to apply a weed killer.

Most individuals prefer their lawns to be as level as possible and without wishing to be prescriptive in establishing a level lawn, the easiest way is to hammer-in pegs over the whole area of the lawn and with the aid of a spirit level, ensure that all the pegs are level, ready to fill with topsoil.

Incidentally, although logical, it may be worth a reminder that a lawn is best prepared and laid during the mild months.

Once the pegs have been removed, and before actually sowing or laying the turf, the surface soil should be raked gently and any stones and weeds should be removed and any large lumps of soil should be broken up.

In order to give your lawn the very best chance it is a very good idea to fertilise the soil with a high phosphate and low nitrogen fertiliser.

The next stage is comparatively easy and is simply firming the area of the proposed lawn, either by tramping it down or using the head of a rake or possibly a board. It is not a good idea to use a heavy roller when preparing the ground because compacting the soil will affect the lawn's ability to drain and may create a soggy lawn after rain.

A Lawn from Seed

A lawn created from seed rather than turf is by far the most cost-effective method. The main thing to bear in mind is what sort of grass you need. If this is going to be a lawn which, for instance, has children running around on it playing games, that is to say grass which is going to have heavy use, it is best to choose a hard wearing ryegrass or one of the numerous hard wearing hybrid varieties which are available nowadays.

However, if your lawn is purely decorative and the only wear it's going to get is when you walk up and down with your lawnmower, it is best to use what are called bent grasses or fescues.

The main difficulty amateur gardeners have is knowing how to go about sowing seed evenly and being able to avoid the lack of seed on one part of the garden, and too much on another part. In the long term, this of course does not matter because grass creates its own carpet-structure and spreads naturally and evenly but as a rough guide, you will need about 35 to 40g of seeds per square metre of lawn.

The best way to proceed here is to work out the area of the lawn and then decide on the total amount of seed that you need before you sieve it onto the grass. If you wish, it is quite effective to simply scatter it by hand, but a sieve gives you a far more even spread.

If you buy your seed in proprietary bags they will tell you exactly what sort of weight of grass you have and what sort of area it will cover. The thing to remember is that sowing grass is not an exact science. So if you overdo it, or perhaps don't have quite enough, don't panic, because grass is very forgiving.

When you are happy that you've dispersed the seed to the best of your ability, all you need now is to sieve a fine layer of soil over the seed, otherwise it would be blown about by the wind and if you anticipate any problems from birds, it is also a good idea to put some bird deterrent over the seed. Some people use a fine mesh net but if your lawn is of a certain size it may be a good idea to simply put in sticks with something shiny attached that the wind will move around, ranging from bits of shiny paper to old CDs or DVDs!

If you talk to your local garden centre or supplier they can advise you on the best sort of grass to use and you are most likely to end up with the general purpose type of mixture, which contains a selection of Rostock meadow grass and smooth stalked meadow grass, plus some fine varieties.

It may be up to 6 months before you have a proper usable lawn, so if you sow your lawn during the mild months when it is comparatively dry, you will find that the wet season will be ideal for the lawn to establish itself. Plus it will save you the problem of constantly watering. In addition if, in spite of all for your efforts, small weeds begin to poke through your new lawn, they will be far easier for you to deal with during the wet months rather than the Summer months.

It won't be long before you see a green haze over what used to be the soil and because the grass at this stage will be quite thin and weak, keep off it! Unless, of course, there is a major weed problem, but even that will take care of itself once you start cutting the grass.

It may sound a little bit 'previous' to mention grass cutting at this stage, but all I will say is that you should only cut the grass when it is as high as 8 cm. There are two things to remember about your lawnmower and that is when cutting brand-new grass, the blade has to be sharp and the height of your cut has to be such that you only trim the tops of the grass, back to say roughly 6 cm. Do not attempt to cut it right back as you would once the lawn has matured... and it may sound obvious, but remember that the soil that the lawn is growing in at the moment is comparatively soft so do choose a dry day before placing a lawnmower on your lawn... and also remember to definitely use the grass box for these early cuts so that you catch the clippings and don't have them cluttering up the soil and affecting drainage and aeration.

You'll be pleased to hear that after two or three initial cuts, most of the weeds will disappear as they do not enjoy having their heads cut off as much as the grass. At this stage, of course, any remaining weeds can still be pulled up by hand.

Turfing a Lawn

We've now had a look at establishing a lawn using seed. Although much cheaper than laying a carpet of turf you have to wait several months until you can enjoy your sown lawn. The great advantage of turfing a lawn is the fact that you are ready to enjoy your new garden feature within weeks.

The groundwork which you need to prepare prior to laying the grass is on a par with what you have to do to seed it.

Measure the area where you want to turf and calculate how many square metres you have. Add a little bit for wastage and then preferably go and inspect the grass that you are going to buy. As you realise, nowadays it is extremely easy to order most things online, but with grass, you need to make sure that you are buying exactly what you are paying for.

The turfs need to be even, they need to hold together, be up to about 40 mm thick and weed free. You can only guarantee that if you go along and have a look at the garden centre shop or farm from which you intend to purchase.

Before you order the turf, and especially if you are going to be covering a reasonably large area, make sure that you have somewhere flat to store it. Try to avoid using the actual soil on which you are going to be laying the turf because you need to leave that as undisturbed as possible.

There are only two tools that you need to lay a good lawn. The first is a plank for you to stand on and the most efficient tool with which to cut turfs to size is an old breadknife.

Individual turfs are laid in a staggered brickwork pattern so that the joints are staggered and all you need to do is start at one edge, lay the first line of turf, place your plank along the newly laid turf and lay the next row. The job itself is very straightforward and before you know it you will have laid the last turf!

When the turf is delivered to your property or wherever it is that you are laying the grass, make sure that you lay the turf within, say, one week of receiving it. Use it before it starts to turn yellow and rooting into itself.

Unlike sowing seeds, the best time to lay turf is in the cooler months, but not when there is a possibility of frost. The reason you should be laying in the slightly damp and cooler months is that turf is very prone to drying out until it actually bonds with the subsoil. Damp or wet weather is obviously the best to prevent your new lawn from drying out and the turf curling up at the edges.

When you have laid your turfs, it's a good idea to lightly roll into place and water them in.

The turf will be delivered to you in strips of about 1000 x 300 mm and when you lay them, you need to butt them together as closely as possible, although when you have finished there is another process we shall be describing to close up any gaps.

When cutting the grass with your breadknife, especially two separate pieces of turf which you want to match exactly, overlap one on top of the other and cut through both of them. Then discard the short bit from the top and the short bit from underneath. You will have a perfect join.

Remember before you start laying and during laying, you must never step on the ground that you have prepared otherwise you'll end up with small indentations in your lawn. You must also make absolutely sure that each turf makes proper contact with the ground underneath.

As far as the edges of the lawn go don't worry about those now and be prepared to leave it looking untidy for a few days until you trim it. If you feel you want to have a neat looking lawn from day one, use your plank as a guide and cut the edges with your knife.

When cutting your new lawn, exactly the same rules apply as to a sown lawn… don't be in too much of a hurry and cut very little off to start with. Before you place a mower on the grass, look carefully at the lawn and if you can still spot the separate turfs, try lifting the corner of one of them off the ground. If it lifts easily it hasn't rooted properly, so leave it alone for a few more days. The last thing you want to do is to break up the new turf with overambitious mowing.

Once again, make sure that you have a grass box on your mower. Although there is some merit to the argument that leaving short cuttings on your lawn means that many nutrients are recycled back into the soil. It also helps to spread unwanted weeds and various diseases. It is generally accepted that it is better to remove the cuttings in the grass box and compost them.

Also, a reminder about rolling your grass. If you do roll, make sure you use a reasonably lightweight roller otherwise you are inhibiting both the root development and the drainage.

Keep an eye on the turfs, especially if you forgot to water and the individual turfs begin to shrink and gaps appear. Don't panic and simply take handfuls of fine soil and put them between the blocks of turf and brush them in with a stiff brush – but do it as gently as possible.

The main thing that you need to remember is that all grasses are very tough and even if you see the odd yellow patch on your new lawn, it will eventually disappear.

Although I have already mentioned the various types of grass that you can use to construct a lawn it is also worth discussing with your supplier, especially if parts of your lawn are very shaded. You may find that he recommends a specific type of grass, especially if you intend to put a lawn underneath, say trees. That can produce extra problems for the grass in that it can be both in the shade and therefore be wetter and also suffer from 'drip' from tree branches.

Renovating an Old Lawn

You may have moved into a new house where the garden was neglected and the lawn looks like a disaster area or you yourself may have abandoned your lawn for several years and done very little to it, apart from looking at it, and occasionally cutting it. This could mean either digging the whole thing up and starting again, or possibly attempting to restore the lawn back to its former glory. Very often the restoration is certainly cheaper and surprisingly much more effective than you might imagine.

You may be looking at something which used to be a lawn and now looks like a bomb site or a piece of waste ground, but remember that the root system is very tough and may well be hiding underneath the surface waiting for you to revive it.

So whether the problem is weeds, damaged grass or just the lawn starved of nutrition, let's have a look at how you might go about turning an old lawn into a new one.

If what used to be a lawn has completely bald patches without any sign of life (and there aren't too many of those), it may be an idea to simply cut away the area to a depth of say 30 to 40 mm, fill the hole with soil, gradually compacting and adding more soil until you are level with the surrounding surfaces. Then simply sow grass seed, followed by a mixture of soil and peat over the seed and then the usual anti-bird protection.

That is how to deal with the odd patch However, if your lawn looks completely worn out with say, a mixture of moss and weeds and very little grass and what is there grows too slowly, rather than digging it all up and starting again, it may be a good idea to try treating the patch with fertiliser after scarification. Then try both weed killer and an anti-moss product. You may find the results quite surprising, especially if there is a residual grassroots system.

You will pleased to know that you can buy kits – so-called 'patch kits' which contain grass seed mixed with compost.

Looking at the opposite end of the spectrum, you may be have a lawn where the grass has grown to half a metre in height and looks like a wasteland. What used to be a lawn resembles a field or meadow.

The first thing you should do is cut the grass down to about 50 mm. If the grass is really long, a normal domestic mower is not suitable for the job and you may have to do it either by hand, with a scythe, a strimmer or even shears. Make sure that you remove the mown grass and once again apply a good dressing of fertiliser. Over the next few weeks, keep decreasing the length of the grass until you achieve about 20 mm or maybe even slightly less. If necessary, apply selective weed killer but not until you are back to what resembles a proper lawn. Once the length of the grass is 'lawn-like', it is a good time for some scarification – which I shall explain in detail later.

Having said all that about renovating a lawn, if you have inherited a lawn, whether good or bad, never be afraid to stamp your own style on any garden. You may well decide to take up all or part of the lawn and perhaps create a new flowerbed instead. If you do decide to do that, make sure that you not only dig up the lawn, but also kill off any grass properly otherwise you will have grass growing up in your new flowerbed.

If the ground has been lawned for over two years, the soil will have an excellent structure for planting with the old roots providing fibre and an existing population of worms will have turned the soil quite comprehensively. Also be aware that old grass areas will also have quite a population of other soil pests which may end up munching their way through the roots of your newly-planted flowers and shrubs.

Never attempt to renovate a lawn in the Summer months, but months where there is some expectation of rain and when the soil is moist. If you attempt any garden restoration in a drought or when the sun is at its highest, you are very unlikely to be as successful as you would be in the damp months. If, for instance, you attempt to dig a square patch of lawn for replacement, you can understand the logic of being able to mark it and cut it in one-piece rather than the several pieces you would get if the undersoil was dry.

Mending little hills and hollows in the lawn, as well as broken edges will be covered in a later chapter – but the general message is that it is worth attempting to renovate an old lawn before reseeding or replacing the turf.

Chapter 2 – Feeding a Lawn and Keeping It Healthy

If your lawn is more of a meadow rather than a neatly manicured patch of grass, then you are very lucky. All you have to do is look at it because that is grass in its natural state, and it can look after itself.

As I mentioned earlier there are those who are lawn fanatics who will tend their lawn as if it was a delicate rose. They will feed it the best fertilisers, they will brush it, edge it, and only step on it to maintain it, but this book is for normal lawn fans rather than the lawn obsessives who maintain their lawn at competition standard for 365 days of the year.

Whatever you do to your lawn it is very unlikely to end up looking like the 18th green at Augusta, but it is comparatively easy to create a very pleasing imitation!

Lawns not only take a lot of mechanical damage in the sense of people walking all over them all the time, but if you think about it, they are the *most* cut plant in the whole garden. Therefore it stands to logic that with all that punishment they will need slightly more nutrition than the rest of the garden and they will need it on a more regular basis. Many lawns are cut every week or two during the seasons when the ground is comparatively warm and are not usually cut at all during cold months.

Feeding a lawn with fertiliser is usually done just before the hot season when the real cutting and mechanical damage begins in earnest. But some lawn aficionados will feed their grass every month and some even more frequently than that.

If you see a lawn which is constantly looking lush and green, assume that the owner is a bit of a lawn fanatic to whom the lawn is no more than a beautiful plant and it's almost certainly a case of 'keep off the grass'.

I shall try and avoid proprietary names of products with which to treat your lawn, but if you remember that for the mild and warm season grasses, fertilisers or feeds tend to be highly in nitrogen, whereas after the warm seasons, the care of the lawn moves from 'the top' when you want it looking lush and green to the roots. The colder seasons are when you apply fertilisers which are high in potash and phosphates so that the roots can beef up for the following warmer seasons.

The main rule is to use a specific grass fertiliser rather than a general garden fertiliser in order to achieve the very best results.

Nowadays it is quite common for people to be concerned about using chemicals in their garden, preferring the organic route and nowadays there are many organic fertilisers available. Many are not as powerful as chemically produced fertilisers which may mean that feeding your lawn can become a year-round (monthly) routine.

Be careful with chemical fertilisers, especially if the weather is comparatively dry because they can sit above the surface and 'scorch' your grass. If you are not sure then use an organic product, although it does not achieve such fast results, it will release nutrients into the grass more slowly.

Depending on the brand, fertilisers can be in liquid or granular form which you can either scatter over the grass or dissolve into a watering can and apply by hand.

There is another product which you can make yourself and which is often used by professional gardeners and that is Lawn Sand. This is a mixture which contains a bit of everything. It is best used in the warmer months, preferably in dry weather but only onto a moist soil.

Lawn Sand contains a mixture of fertiliser and weed killer but must not be applied heavily because once again, you can scorch your grass. The mixtures vary and you can also buy it ready mixed, but the mixture is approximately 80% silver sand, 16% sulphate of ammonia and 4% sulphate of iron. Whenever you are gardening, remember that we are practising 'bucket chemistry'. So whether you're slightly out on the mixture it will not particularly matter, because those are the rough proportions by weight.

You need to allow air to get to the grass and soil all year round so to make sure that if you have leaves on your grass, you remove them as soon as possible before they rot. Not only are you preventing sunlight getting to your grass but rotting vegetation does encourage all sorts of pests.

It is just not true that allowing leaves and other detritus to compost into the lawn somehow does it any good. The opposite is true.

Feeding alone is not just about applying chemicals because the very best substance that you can ever apply to a lawn is water. The only thing you need to remember with water is that it is done properly and not overdone.

If the lawn is really dry, wait until evening and give it a really good soaking. Then leave it for a few days before soaking it again. That is much more beneficial than 24/7 sprinkling.

Many of the varieties of grass that are used for lawns – such as fescues and bents are what are known as poverty grasses. That means that they originated from areas of low fertility. You cannot really go wrong whatever watering and fertilising regime you decide on.

If you have the type of lawn which is purely ornamental, that is to say it has a very fine grass and doesn't have deckchairs, hordes of children or barbecues on it, you may find that you only have to fertilise it once every few years.

If your lawn is of the average type, where children play, etc it will benefit from being fed much more often – which means at least once every year so.

All you really need to know is that the chief mineral which a grass needs is nitrogen, such as that contained in sulphate of ammonia.

Distributing fertiliser can be achieved simply by spreading by hand. You can mix it with a compost which acts as a spreading agent and in order to achieve an even distribution, the best method is to spread up and down the lawn, followed by across.

Needless to say, there are proprietary fertiliser distributors. They come in two types. One is a linear distributor which distributes the fertiliser by a roller or a spinner. Neither has any advantage over the other. The other distributes laterally. Once again the best thing to do is to go to your local garden centre or supplier and talk to an expert.

If you are using machinery to spread fertiliser, the good news is that you don't have to mix it with compost and it is applied to the lawn. 'neat'.

You may come across the term 'top dressing'. Usually and generally in horticulture, top dressing means applying fertiliser to the surface of the soil. In the context of lawns the term means adding some sort of mixture of sand, peat and topsoil – usually applied with a sieve to further feed the lawn. Again top dressing can be bought ready mixed.

There are occasions when the topsoil of the lawn becomes so compacted that the lawn will start to hold water – that is to say, visible wet patches. The answer is proper aeration. It is nowadays possible to buy a proper aerator which is basically a load of spikes on a cylinder which you push along and it make holes in the lawn at measured intervals. If you are feeling up to it, the same can be achieved with a garden fork. It is good practice to carry out this process every two or three years anyway, whether your lawn is showing excess water or not.

Chapter 3 – Lawn Pests and How to Deal with Them

'Pests' which affect the health of the lawn can be animal, vegetable or mineral and confirm the old adage that gardening is no more than a constant and ongoing battle with nature. If a lawn or indeed a garden were left to their own devices, nature would gradually return it to the wild state. Part of the battle to prevent this is to fight the pests which constantly attack our garden. The lawn is particularly susceptible to various pests and predators ranging from weeds to burrows made in lawns by bumblebees. Let's start with the weeds.

The type of weed that you are likely to see invading your lawn very much depends on not only the lawn surroundings but also on the type of grass and the moisture within the lawn, as well as whether it is shady or exposed to sunlight.

Most weeds respond to chemicals of one sort or another with the only alternative being on one's hands and knees, cutting the offending weed out. Unfortunately, when removing a weed by hand it is practically impossible to remove the entire root system which means that it is inevitable that the weed will return.

For instance, a common weed found on lawns is clover. Some individuals find this very attractive and in fact attempt to cultivate it as it does produce a very good ground cover, spreads quickly and requires little mowing. Luckily, if you are not a big fan, it is very susceptible to certain chemicals such as Ioxynil which will kill it.

However, even with a regular application of such a chemical, it will take time to produce permanent results.

Damp lawns are very susceptible to moss invasion. Having said that, moss has been known to invade bumps on the lawn where the mower has not only removed all the grass but also its roots. The very best way to avoid moss growing on your lawn is to produce good healthy grass on a well-drained surface. The so-called selective weed killers, which contain plant growth suppressors are very effective when moss or indeed most of the weeds are growing, but this defence is only marginally more effective than attacking it with a metal lawn rake.

If you do decide to treat moss on your lawn, a good starting point is to establish why it is present, because unless you identify the cause and deal with it, it is most likely to return very quickly.

You may discover discolouration on your lawn, especially when the lawn begins to dry. Not the normal discolouration, but the type which looks very yellow and remains yellow, no matter how much water is put onto it.

If your lawn is in the vicinity of trees, these yellow patches may be caused by fungus, which is associated with tree roots. This fungus turns the soil in its vicinity into an almost impermeable membrane which effectively waterproofs the soil, meaning that the grassroots will receive minimal moisture no matter how hard they are watered.

You can either go to your gardening shop or buy a proprietary product called a soil penetrant which is diluted and put onto the soil. The substance which has waterproofed the soil is then dissolved and dissipated... or you can take a garden fork and spike the soil, breaking through the waterproof sections, thus allowing the grassroots exposure to water and nutrients.

The fungus associated with tree roots is not to be confused with what is known as yellow tuft disease, the cause of which is still unknown. It occurs mostly in grass which is constantly damp. However, it has been shown that scarification does the trick. This disease is most likely to be caused by another variety of fungus.

Lawn grass conditions are extremely attractive to a whole variety of fungus, ranging from the highly visible mushrooms to the mysterious fairy rings. It can be treated with chemicals or if it is a real problem, the best method is to dig out the offending patch, fill it with soil, seed it and start again.

Earlier I mentioned sulphate of ammonia as a lawn dressing, which confirms that prevention is much better than cure. For instance, lawn problems such as Corticium Disease. If some of your grass become pink and red and your lawn takes an overall appearance of a mottled brown colour, it is most certainly the victim of Corticium. Although it can look alarming, the grass is almost never killed, but the disease does respond extremely well to a light dressing of sulphate of ammonia. In extreme cases, you can apply a specific fungicide.

Needless to say, the bigger weeds are easy to deal with – you can simply dig them up! But if you do, make sure that you not only remove every last bit of root but that you dispose of the weeds on a compost heap.

Earthworm casts are quite visible on a close-cropped lawn and although unsightly can simply be brushed into the grass because the presence of earthworms is always useful because they do keep the soil aerated, mixed and healthy. Earthworm casts can be unsightly and gardeners consider them particularly good for attracting and holding onto weed seeds and that is the primary reason (apart from their appearance) why they should be removed.

If you leave your grass cuttings on the lawn surface, that will encourage earthworm activity. However, if you are having a problem with earthworms, there are several poisons which will kill them. For instance permanganate of potash will bring the worms to the surface so that you can deal with them. But there are all sorts of propriety products on the market, which also promise to deal with earthworm issues. On balance, however, earthworms are usually considered quite beneficial. Their habit of creating new drainage channels in the lawn subsoil, as well as pulling organic matter below ground really does help with enriching soil. In general, if you have earthworms present in and around your lawn, it is a sure sign of a healthy lawn.

There is one lawn pest which tends not to be regarded as beneficial to your lawn. It is the lava of the crane fly and is known as the leather jacket – because of its appearance. If you spot flocks of starlings on your lawn, picking away at grubs, it is a sure sign that crane flies have been laying eggs. It is quite easy to deal with any starling damage to your lawn, so there are occasions when the best policy is to let nature take its course.

Cockchafer grubs are another pest which enjoy attacking turf. They can be also be eradicated with the appropriate chemical... but once again, if you keep, keep your lawn reasonably short and leaf free, birds will help you with all grubby problems.

Another so-called lawn pest is the bee. However, I am certainly not going to recommend that you even think about poisoning bees. They will dig a small hole in the grass (especially on an untended lawn with longer than average grass!). The queen bee enters the nest which it has excavated and eventually you may see it flying in and out. Below ground, there are several small cells in which she rears her young. If you have bee holes in your lawn, it should encourage you to keep your grass shorter or at least switch your mower on occasionally because it is a vibrating ground, which they don't appreciate. They only like undisturbed lawns and really only represent a call to action to you.

If you have little hillocks in your lawn which had been shaved clean of grass by your lawnmower blade, and you have a period of hot weather, you are likely to notice a sudden influx of ants. They like to build their nests in dry, hot soil and you're most likely to spot them during the Summer. The ant cure is deceptively simple – soak the soil. Alternatively, you can treat in the same way that you treat the bees – leave them alone. By the end of the Summer they grow wings and fly away. Sometimes it is best to allow nature to take its course, rather than to fight it!

Another very good reason for attempting to control your lawns earthworm population is the potential presence of that most disruptive of lawn pests – the mole. The classic signs of a mole infestation are those little soil hillocks, which are the points at which the mole emerges for a breath of fresh air and then burrows down again in his quest for earthworms. Moles are not urban dwellers and the most likely place to find them is in the countryside. In the old days, all sorts of schemes and chemicals were devised to deal with a mole infestation, but the general feeling nowadays is to live with it until they move on. Cures such as tipping poison into their tunnels or attempting to gas them has never been shown to be particularly effective. The only semi-effective deterrent has only been on the market for a few years and that is the electronic mole repellent which you stick in the ground and it makes a low-frequency vibrating noise.

The good news is that in your career as a gardener or lawn keeper, you are extremely unlikely to ever suffer from a mole infestation.

So the general rule in dealing with lawn pests, is if it's vegetable kill it. If it's animal, try to live with it.

If it is your dog urinating on the lawn, creating those large yellow patches by far the best solution is to take it for a walk!

Chapter 4 – The Four Seasons

It may be scary to think that in order to have a decent lawn, you need to be out there for the entire year, holding bugs and diseases at bay just to have a decent patch of grass in your garden. It's not as frightening as it sounds because in actual fact, the amount of time you need to dedicate to your lawn is only a fraction of the time you should be allocating to your shrubs, flowers, decking, rockery and all the other paraphernalia of gardening.

I propose that we go season by season, starting with Spring. Let's face it, the only time you are going to be actively using your lawn is most likely to be the Summer and part of Spring. Autumn and Winter (the time when most lawns stop growing) are the times of the year when lawn work slows down, and obviously during the Winter months, tends to grind to a halt.

You won't be surprised to learn that the longest section in this chapter is:

Spring

What you do to your lawn in Spring will set the tone for the rest of the year. If you spend a good amount of time and maximum effort during the Spring months, you will be assured of a decent lawn all the way through the year to the following Spring.

The grass itself probably enjoys the Spring more than any time of year. It is when it wakes up after Winter and begins to grow in earnest. These are the times when gradually your grass is going to need more and more water as well as feed.

However, some parts of the world have notoriously unreliable weather, which means that you can be caught out by assuming that Winter is over. You start sowing seeds and then there's the hard frost. Not only making the ground as workable as a rock, it can also kill your seeds. So make sure that Spring has arrived properly before you venture onto your grass.

In an earlier chapter we mentioned creating a new lawn either from turf or from seed and Spring is the ideal time to begin the process. At this time of year the sun is beginning to climb higher in the sky, it is more pleasant to be outside, but more importantly the soil itself is gradually beginning to warm up and if you sow seeds, the rain or more importantly, the mixture of sun and rain, will help the seeds germinate.

If you want to establish a lawn for you to use during the Summer, laying turf at this time of year is a good idea because of the decreased risk of frost.

Some will tell you that Winter is the good time to be laying turf and in principle there is no problem with that, but if your soil is *really* cold it can be a bit difficult to prepare the undersoil properly and obtaining decent turf in the Winter is usually quite a problem, as is the risk of frost. The advice therefore is to be patient and wait until Spring.

In these days of climate change, the rules appear to be different to the way they were. Several years ago, traditionally, Spring used to be the time when grass started to grow. Nowadays it is quite common for grass to start growing during the Winter when the soil is not only wet but the ground has begun to warm up far too early.

Once again, the general rule is to be patient and not to place your lawnmower on the grass until the lawn has at least partially dried out.

If you think about gardening science, you may be interested to know that the optimum soil type, for grass growth has a pH of about 6.5. That is to say, the soil is more or less neutral on the acid-alkaline scale.

You can buy a soil testing very cheaply. And if you are inclined to do so, take a couple of samples of soil from in and around your lawn and measure the pH. If the soil is too acidic or too alkaline, go to your garden centre and ask about the appropriate additives to return the soil to neutrality. In fact, some garden suppliers will do a free soil test for you if you go along with a sample. It all depends on how green and how lush you want your lawn to be.

The reason I mentioned testing is because far too many people will throw handfuls of lime onto the grass or the wrong kind of additive purely because they feel that they should. You can save yourself a lot of money if you confirm the pH of your soil and that it has the correct amount of potassium and phosphorus.

Once you've established that, all you have to do is feed your lawn with a nitrogen rich fertiliser and you are good to go!

Now that we have finished the scientific bit, it is a good time to remember that yes, it is very easy to become involved in all the scientific aspects of gardening but in the case of grass it can stand a huge volume of neglect. If you are the sort of gardener who simply wants a patch of grass and all the equipment you feel is necessary, are a lawnmower and a spade for edging, don't worry.

Speaking of lawnmowers… if you want to wake up your lawn in the Spring and the ground isn't too soft, by all means get your mower out and go for it! No matter what the lawn looks like before you give it a light cut, it will look far better after the process.

If you want to use your mower as a vacuum cleaner to dispose of leaves and other detritus on your lawn just set your blades above cut height and mow. You can do that at any time of year!

Once you give your lawn the very first Springtime mow, be warned… it will wake up. Once you start cutting grass, it sits up, takes notice and starts to try and stay ahead of you and your mower.

During Spring weeds begin to germinate and stick their heads up above the ground. Weed controlled by a mower is an excellent way to keep them in check.

We haven't yet mentioned edging or trimming your lawn and there are two schools of thought. The first is edge before you mow and the other is (obviously) mow before you edge. Personally, I prefer edging first, leaving the trimmings on the grass and then mowing.

During your first Springtime mow you may be wondering whether or not you should attach the basket to your lawnmower in order to catch the cuttings. The general rule of thumb is that if your grass is ridiculously long because you totally neglected it from late Summer, don't be frightened to take one or two cuts, but don't leave the cuttings on the grass. If, however, you have been diligent enough to start with a reasonably short lawn, it doesn't matter if you take your first cut without the basket and leave the cuttings on the grass.

However, that only applies if you don't have a very dense lawn as a result of previously leaving clippings on the surface. In that case you will need to start the soil breathing again and Springtime is a good time to rake the lawn clean using either a normal lawn rake or if you prefer a power 'dethatcher'.

Spring is also a good time to check for bumps and hollows in your lawn and as most professional gardeners are not very keen on the idea of rolling, removing bumps and hollows becomes a manual job. Don't be afraid to cut out a slight bump in the lawn, and removing any excess soil. Obviously the converse applies to any hollows. The way **not** to deal with any slightly higher bits on the lawn (no matter why they are there) is to stamp on them. That will only create soil compaction and future drainage problems.

I have briefly mentioned that perennial problem all gardeners have with weeds. With modern weed killers it is now possible to deal with each weed individually. In the case of weeds such as dandelion, it may well worth you spraying each individual plant as soon as its leaves appear. That way you will kill it way down to the root.

Summer

After a very busy Spring tending your lawn the ambition should be to spend the Summer months admiring the lawn and using it.

Unfortunately though, the hot Summer months are when the grass and weeds and everything else get into high gear and grow at their fastest rate.

It seems counterintuitive, but the Summer months are also the time when you water at the highest rate which further encourages the grass and weeds to grow. Regrettably, there is no easy solution. Summer is the time of mowing and watering.

Walking on a very dry lawn is not a good idea because the abrasive action of dry soil as you walk on it will damage the grass. That means that the lawn needs to be kept reasonably damp because as the Summer temperature increases, and especially if the sun is really hot, you need to water your lawn every few days.

If you decide to give your lawn a good soaking, do it in the evening when the sun is on its way down. That way, water will soak into your lawn overnight. If you water during the day when the ground is hard the water will simply run off and evaporate.

There will be times when you cannot keep up with damage caused by the heat of the sun. For instance, you may go on holiday and leave the lawn unattended for a few weeks returning to a straw coloured field. If that does happen, simply water the grass. As mentioned before, it takes more than a few weeks without water to kill a root system so although there will be occasions when your lawn looks pretty horrific, a little bit of patience and watering will soon revive what may have looked like dead grass.

Every time you water a lawn you should be providing roughly 2 to 3 cm of water.

The Summer months are also the time of sprinklers which are a fabulous way of keeping your lawn moist in spite of the sun's attempts to suck the water into the atmosphere. There are no right or wrong rules as far as sprinklers are concerned. Apart from making sure that every part of the lawn has its fair share of moisture.

If there is a prolonged period of hot weather it is a good idea not to mow the grass and to allow it to grow a little bit longer. That way it'll retain moisture. Much easier than if it is scalped down to ground level.

You may also have noticed that a lawn that is very short, produces a much larger than expected volume of weeds during very hot months. That is because weed seeds need lots of light to germinate and of course a very close-cut lawn provides lots of light for them.

So if you have a very hot Summer think about either adjusting your mower blades to say double the height you would normally consider or if you wish, stop mowing altogether.

During the Summer months pay special attention to any straw coloured brown patches on your lawn. They cannot all be blamed on your neighbour's dog or cat and may be the first sign of a fungus infection underneath your grass. If you do suspect some sort of fungal infection don't be frightened to photograph it and take it your local garden centre or dealer for identification. Under no circumstances should you cut out the offending patch of soil and take it with you because fungal spores spread very readily, and your local garden centre will not thank you for arriving with a lump of soil containing several million fungus spores!

You're very unlikely to see many earthworms during the Summer months, except after a heavy watering of your lawn, but as I've said before, earthworms and insects do tend to be lawn friendly so don't worry about them too much.

The only exception to this can be the odd ants nest, especially if you have children. Once again, regular watering can keep ants nests in check, because they favour dry hot soil.

Although all the above sounds a bit onerous, with an average lawn, you're very unlikely to spend more than about an hour per week on lawn maintenance.

Autumn

While you are waiting for Winter, you have quite a few weeks during which to prepare the lawn and undo any obvious damage sustained during the Summer.

This is the time of year when you stop using the lawn and when you can see that the Summer footfall has not only compacted some of the grass, but also some of the subsoil and root system.

This is a good time to give the lawn a cut, followed by a good rake, as well as making holes in the lawn in order to aerate it. If you are using your own equipment, then there's no problem.

However, if you have a larger lawn and are thinking of hiring any sort of machinery in order to scarify the lawn, clean the equipment before you use it. A lot of hire equipment is not cleaned by the supplier as diligently as it should have been. Which means that there is a very real danger of introducing various pests into your lawn. As soon as you take delivery of your mechanical kit from the supplier, hose it down thoroughly.

Depending on where you live, Autumn (or fall!) can be a good time to seed or reseed your grass and horticultural technology nowadays is such that you can even buy grasses specifically bred for the region in which you live. However that's outside the scope of this book, but it may be worth you doing some research on the subject.

We mentioned that one of the most important things for the off-season is to ensure that the lawn is clean. Your grass needs sunlight all the year round and any leaves, twigs, stones, fruit etc are inhibiting the sunlight reaching your grass.

Unfortunately, if you do have trees in your garden, you could not have failed to notice that they all shed their leaves at different times which means keeping your lawn clear is a constant job for at least three months.

Some experts recommend one of those leaf blowers, which will certainly remove leaves from your lawn and deposit them elsewhere. But (and this depends on the size of your lawn), if you are able to, rake the rubbish off your lawn. That way you do two jobs at once... cleaning and scarifying.

Believe it or not, there is now a product called 'Winteriser', otherwise known as a Stage 4 fertiliser. You can spread this over your lawn at this time of year in to allow the grass to rest surrounded by potash etc in order to create a level of disease resistance and improve its stability. Let's just say that fertilising your lawn as the last act before Winter will do no harm.

Winter

You are probably thinking *". There can't possibly be anything to do to my lawn during the Winter months"...* and you're almost right!

If you live in an area where you are likely to see the snow, your lawn decisions will be made for you, especially if your lawn is sitting under several metres of snow.

However, it is all to do with the preparation. The final cut of the year is usually done at the beginning of Winter. Wait until you have a reasonably dry day and then cut the lawn as short as you can. There are several reasons for this, but the most important is that you want to avoid your grass being bent by any weight of snow.

There is not much preparation to do for the Winter except to ensure that the lawn remains clear and free of leaves and all the other paraphernalia of a busy Summer, ranging from children's toys to barbecue scorch marks. Remember that anything that you leave on the lawn over the Winter months can result in patches of dead grass. So the very simple Winter rule is: clear your lawn.

The biggest Winter job for a lawn enthusiast is the cleaning of equipment, but we are going to cover that in the next chapter.

Chapter 5 – Cutting the Lawn

Unless you are stuck in the 1940s you will know that unless your lawn is about 1m², the days of shears, scythes and even rakes have been replaced by machinery. That does not mean you necessarily have to buy expensive electrical or motor driven equipment in order to maintain a decent lawn but sometimes it helps!

Admittedly, some aspects of lawn care are a bit over the top. For instance, we now have the automatic lawnmower which you simply place on the lawn, turn it on and let it go while you continue with the sunbathing. Of course, you can take laboursaving devices to the extreme, so we will have a sensible look at all the equipment available to you in order to maintain your grass in the best possible condition.

For the purposes of this book, I propose that we ignore the robot lawnmowers and concentrate on the three main groups of mower available to us: The hand mower, the motor mower, and the electric mower. Each has its use and both good and bad points.

If you have a tiny suburban or urban lawn, it is hardly worth the trouble of buying a motor mower. The best bet for you is the electric mower or if you're feeling particularly energetic, you can still buy those old-fashioned push along mowers, which nowadays not only look modern but also work much better than those heavy old cast-iron monstrosities of the past.

If you want stripes on your lawn you will need a mower with a roller behind the cutters and for a small lawn, that means a straightforward manual mower is the best.

Electric hover mowers cut grass very well but the vast majority of them, especially the small ones, do not collect the grass. That means an extra job. However, the very large electric ones do have a grass collection box and are by far the fastest way to cut your grass. The big disadvantage with electric mowers is the metres and metres of cable that you end up trailing behind you and those people who have tried and then permanently abandoned electric mowers have probably had the rather unpleasant experience of cutting through their cable. Yes, we know that shouldn't have happened, but it does.

If you decide to go the electric route, simply make sure that you have some sort of current interrupter between the mower cable and your mains socket. So that if you do cut through the cable or come across something which stops the blades, you don't blow all the fuses in your house because the current to the mower will be tripped out. Remember the trip switch!

Most of the work involved in cutting the lawn appears to be the disposal of the grass cuttings. For that reason, try to find a mower with a large grass box. Of course, no system is perfect because if you have a large grass box, you will eventually be pushing something that weighs quite a substantial amount. It's all a question of balance.

The biggest development over the last 20 to 30 years has been in the motor mower. It has gone from being a motorised version of the push mower to a start-from-scratch design all of its own.

The original mowers were huge clunky things with a solid metal grass box on the front which weighed about 30 kilos when it came to emptying and it was altogether most unsatisfactory and probably did more damage to a lawn than a whole Summer of children.

The modern motor mower relies on extremely reliable, lightweight four stroke engines and is not only extremely effective, but reliable to the extent that the owner can totally disregard all the Winterising instructions from the manufacturer, put the mower away at the beginning of Winter and simply turn it on the following Spring. Needless to say, that is not recommended as every motormower needs to be Winterised and cleaned ready for the off season.

Most domestic motor mowers come in two types. The first is the push along type, which usually has a rotary blade (first used in the hover mower) and the second is a slightly heavier design because it has a gearbox which drives the rear wheels so that a lot of the 'push work' is eliminated. This type of mower is particularly useful if you have a sloping garden or if you are, perhaps, of a certain age and can do without pushing a mower up and down the lawn for an hour or two!

As I mentioned before, the passion for stripes on a lawn is gradually disappearing. However, there are now rotary motor mowers which *do* have a roller at the rear, which helps to generate the traditional striped effect.

If you have an absolutely huge lawn, you may wish to invest in one of those mini tractor type ride-on mowers, but their obvious disadvantage is that used too often, they will compact not only the lawn but the substrata as well. However, if you imagine yourself driving a mini tractor around the lawn wearing a straw hat, steering wheel in one hand and a Pina colada in the other, then this may be a good option for you.

This chapter is about cutting the lawn and lawnmowers are certainly not the only cutting equipment that a lawn aficionado uses.

In the pre-electric and pre-motorised days, one of the most important jobs to a really fastidious gardener would be to edge the lawn. You can still purchase those halfmoon spade like diggers which you use to cut around the lawn edge and in spite of all the new electric and petrol strimmers on the market these days, the halfmoon lawn edger is still by far the best way to obtain a really crisp edge to your lawn.

Electric and motor strimmers have been around for a few years now and as prices come down, more and more people are using them not only to cut longer grass and cut weeds down to ground level, but they can be used to trim the edges of the lawn quite effectively. But on the understanding that they do only cut the grass and do not shape the soil. They are a direct substitute for the long-handled shears which many gardeners still prefer.

Let us now have a look at some of the 'best practices' of lawn cutting.

You may think that the primary purpose of cutting the lawn is to control it, but in fact a regular cut will increase the density of your grass as well as keeping weeds in check. Although, for the purposes of this book, it is not of great importance, but the numerous varieties of grasses available have recommended lengths. However, worrying too much about the correct height of a particular grass is not something that I propose to dwell on.

If you stick to the general rule of never cutting more than one third of the grass blade, you cannot go far wrong. Remember that just like any other plant, grass produces its own food through photosynthesis and chopping it right down to the ground makes it almost impossible for it to grow effectively and it would also make it more vulnerable to all the diseases and pests I mentioned in the previous section.

If you have ever tried to mow long wet grass you will know that it is almost impossible because not only does the lawnmower have difficulty in blowing cut grass into the basket, leading to you having to pull out compacted long, wet grass from the mower, but the blades are not actually cutting. Even the sharpest blade cannot get proper purchase on wet grass. The mower is in effect, is *smashing* through the grass and leaving jagged edges rather than a clean cut.

Once again grass with jagged edges will increase pests and diseases.

The rule is only mow when your grass is absolutely dry and keep the mower blades as sharp as you can. A mower blade is normally attached to the engine with a single bolt, making it very easy to take out and sharpen with either a stone or a file.

Long-term cutting in exactly the same direction every time causes your grass to develop a 'lean' in the direction of the cut. If you vary the direction of your cut your grass will always grow vertically, rather than being pushed in a certain direction.

We have already discussed the question of whether or not to leave clippings on the lawn or whether to collect them in the basket and dispose of them. Some will argue that in leaving clippings on a lawn you will be returning nutrients to the soil... and that of course is true, but only do that if you are taking a very fine cut. Leaving longer clippings on the lawn will do nothing apart from creating semi-impermeable thatch which will stifle lawn growth and leave you with another raking job.

If you have areas of shade on your lawn, for instance, under trees, you may notice that the grass which grows in the shade is longer than the grass exposed to full sunlight. Bear that in mind when cutting.

Before you actually drive onto your lawn with either your hover mower or motor mower walk around the lawn and pick up any debris, such as stones and twigs. If you've been mowing and your mower blade has ever hit a stone, you'll already know the dangers of a pebble flying across your garden at 100 kilometres an hour!

It may sound a little bit over the top but manufacturers always recommend that you wear goggles and strong shoes. Remember those blades can be rotating at quite a speed and needless to say, there have been accidents which have resulted in people losing toes. Steel toe capped boots are the best but being conscious that you are working with a potentially dangerous machine is even better.

At the beginning of this chapter I mentioned that modern mowers are so reliable that you can simply put them away without Winterising them. To a large extent that is true, but if you want your mower to last for many years, it is a good idea to clean it, check the plug, keep the oil at the proper level and because a lawnmower tends to vibrate, always check that there are no nuts and bolts which are gradually coming loose.

As far as electric mowers are concerned, you don't have to be told not to cut through the cable and certainly do not attempt to do any work at all on it without properly disconnecting it from the mains. Switching off is certainly not enough.

If you maintain your lawnmower, even in the most basic way it should last you a lifetime.

Chapter 6 – Non-grass Lawns

The dictionary definition of 'lawn' is *'an area of grass which is tended or mowed'* but, believe it or not, a lawn does not have to be grass, although many of the so-called alternative lawns do contain some grass... apart, of course from Astroturf!

For instance, these days there is a move to the less formal garden and a return to nature through a slightly 'wild' look. Many gardeners have moved away from the formality of a tightly shorn square of grass to the much 'looser' meadow look or what is known as a wildflower lawn.

A wildflower lawn looks as if all you will have to do is sit back in your deckchair and look at it, but in fact you can sow a wildflower lawn in exactly the same way that you do a grass lawn.

Your current lawn may already contain the occasional clump of daisies, violets, buttercups or primroses and cowslips and the idea of cultivating a wildflower lawn is simply to encourage these wildflowers to flourish.

A formal grass lawn tends to be a bit of a sterile looking object, whereas a wildflower lawn can be a thing of great beauty which attracts all sorts of insects, ranging from butterflies to a whole array of crawling insects. Such a lawn is you creating a mini ecosystem within your garden.

That does not mean that you will never have to tend it because even a wildflower garden needs to be cut. Occasionally, probably once or twice a year, you can rake it in order to remove dead grass or weeds, although the purist meadow gardener will even encourage the weeds because even some of these are quite beautiful when flowering and will attract their own insect species.

You can even go to your local garden centre and buy a bag of wildflower seeds in order to give yourself a start.

Some convert their traditional lawn into a wildflower garden by planting individual plants on the lawn, as well as seeding it.

Remember there are no rules!

Clover is and one of those plants which many gardeners consider to be a weed, but a clover lawn can be a very attractive looking garden feature, especially if you plant a mixture of clover and grass. It'll still need to be mowed but with the advantage of the clover having the quality of being able to retain nitrogen, thus creating what in effect is a self feeding lawn.

Clover will only grow to a height of 7 to 8 cm with the added advantage of producing small flowers which will attract all sorts of insects, especially bees. The clover lawn will give you the best of both worlds... a semi-wild lawn with the added attraction of less mowing and less fertilisation.

The classic non-grass lawn, of course, is the camomile, made famous and romanticised by Mary Wesley in her 1984 novel.

A camomile lawn not only produces very tight groundcover, but by doing so, inhibits the growth of weeds, plus it has its own special perfume.

One of the great traditional enemies of the traditional lawn gardener is moss. He will be found studying the grass carefully and any outbreak of moss will be immediately dispatched with a lawn rake!

However, some modern gardeners have embraced moss because it makes very attractive groundcover, especially in darker shaded areas and once established, requires very little maintenance. So a moss lawn is also worth considering.

You can see, therefore, that although we understand 'lawn' to mean grass, there is an infinite number of ways of creating your own custom lawn. All you need is a plot of land and lots of imagination.

Conclusion

I have always considered the lawn to be a very spiritual place which combines physical activity, technical knowledge, as well as giving one the ability to appreciate the aesthetics and mysteries of nature.

I have already mentioned that gardening in general tends to be a constant battle against nature, but with a lawn it is possible to achieve a truce with nature and through that a harmony and an understanding.

Yes, of course, if *all* you want to see on your lawn is grass and nothing but grass, you will of course be embarking on a year-round battle. But if you back off just a little bit and for instance allow those little bee tunnels in the grass and maybe the odd ants nest or daisy, you will be on the way to achieving what I believe to be the purpose of cultivation... and that is a goodwill *towards* and empathy *with* nature.

Just a small area of grass can not only give you an interest but certainly improve the quality of your life.

This book is giving you ways of tending and looking after a lawn and an opportunity to learn *everything* there is to know about a very small section of horticulture but with added health (exercise) and both spiritual and intellectual benefits.

Think of your lawn almost as a pet. Yes, it can look after itself and does so for most of the time but if you want it to behave and you want to derive the maximum benefit from it, you can tend it, feed it and spoil it, so that you both derive the maximum pleasure.

This is not a gardening book for gardeners... you will have noticed that I have not been prescriptive at any time because it is up to you as an individual to stamp your own personality on how you look after your lawn.

However, you will have noticed that I have not gone overboard on what I call the 'OCD lawn' which is so perfect that it causes its owner untold stress, especially when someone dares to step on it!

But having a regular, flat, green, lush imperfection-free lawn is important to some people and there is nothing wrong with that... but that defeats the object of what I have been trying to describe which is to work with nature and enjoy the natural aspects of your lawn rather than regarding it as a conflict.

Looking after a lawn can be frustrating and confusing and if you read the conventional gardening books you will understand exactly what I mean. That is why I have avoided all Latin names, chemical formulae etc because most of us are not scientists or gardening scholars.

I sincerely hope that this book has fired your imagination to some extent, giving you the tools to at least think about your lawn in a slightly different way.

If you don't yet possess a lawn, I assure you that you have a great deal to look forward to.